D0069272

Henry Ford

History Maker Bios

Jeffrey Zuehlke

BARNES & NOBLE

NEW YORK

Text © 2007 by Lerner Publications Company
Illustrations © 2007 by Lerner Publications Company

This 2007 edition published by Barnes & Noble, Inc.
by arrangement with Lerner Publications Company, a division of
Lerner Publishing Group, Minneapolis, MN.

Illustrations by Big Time Attic

Barnes & Noble, Inc.
122 Fifth Avenue
New York, NY 10011

ISBN-13: 978-0-7607-8191-3
ISBN-10: 0-7607-8191-5

Printed and bound in the United States of America

1 3 5 7 9 10 8 6 4 2

Table of Contents

INTRODUCTION

Many people think Henry Ford invented the automobile. He didn't. He was just one of many inventors to build a car in the 1890s. But years later, Henry built a very special car. It was called the Model T. It was the first car that the average American could afford.

The Model T changed the way Americans lived. When Henry was born, the United States was a country of farmers. Most people didn't travel much. And when they did, they rode in trains or horse-drawn wagons.

By the time Henry died, more than half of all Americans lived in cities. They traveled in fast cars along paved streets. Henry helped bring about that change. Along the way, he became one of the world's richest and most famous men.

This is his story.

1 NATURAL-BORN MECHANIC

Henry Ford was born on July 30, 1863. He grew up in a farming community near Dearborn, Michigan.

Henry's father, William Ford, was a farmer. He had moved to the United States from Ireland sixteen years earlier. William was a serious and hardworking man.

Henry's mother, Mary Litogot O'Hern Ford, had grown up in a wealthy family. Mary was a kind but stern parent. She expected Henry and his five younger brothers and sisters to work hard around the farm.

Mary Ford believed in doing chores well, with little wasted effort. "She was . . . orderly and thorough," Henry later recalled. "And she demanded that from us."

William Ford (LEFT) and Mary Litogot O'Hern Ford (RIGHT) lived on a large and successful farm.

Henry grew up in this farmhouse.

Henry didn't like to do his chores. Henry's neighbor described him as "the laziest bugger on the face of the earth. . . . Henry would work along all right until about ten o'clock in the morning, and then he would go to the house for a drink of water. . . . But he would never come back!"

Henry believed farming took too much effort. He was always looking for easier ways to do things. "Even when [I was] very young," he said, "I suspected that much might be done in a better way."

Henry had a talent for fixing things. As a schoolboy, he became known for his skill at mending watches. He spent much of his time in the classroom repairing timepieces he kept hidden in his desk.

Machines fascinated Henry. He loved to take things apart and study them. "When we had . . . toys given to us at Christmas," remembered Henry's sister, "we always said, 'Don't let Henry see them! He'll take them apart!'"

EXPERIMENTING

Young Henry was always experimenting. "There is [a lot] to be learned simply by tinkering with things," Henry once wrote. But not all of his experiments went smoothly. Once he sealed the whistle hole on a teakettle. He wanted to see what would happen when the water came to a boil. The kettle exploded. Hot water and pieces of metal flew everywhere. Henry ended up with a cut on his cheek.

Sometimes Henry would walk ten miles to Detroit just to snoop around in hardware stores. In the 1870s, the city was becoming a hub for industry. It was home to many factories and workshops.

One day, Henry was traveling to Detroit with his father. As they rode in their wagon, they saw a strange machine chugging down the road. It was a steam-powered vehicle. Henry had never seen anything like it. "I was off the wagon and talking to the engineer before my father . . . knew what I was up to," Henry later recalled.

Steam-powered cars were a fad in the 1870s.

In addition to cars, steam engines powered stagecoaches like this one.

The excited boy peppered the driver with questions about the machine. Henry listened closely as the engineer explained how the engine worked. It created power by burning coal. The burning coal produced steam inside a boiler. The steam created power to spin a wheel. A belt connected the spinning wheel to the rear wheels of the vehicle. "It was the first vehicle other than horse-drawn that I had ever seen," said Henry.

The experience changed Henry's life. His thoughts soon revolved around "making a machine that would travel the roads."

Henry realized that he wouldn't be able to do such a thing living on a farm. The country offered few opportunities for studying machines. Henry decided to move away. In 1879, sixteen-year-old Henry left his father's farm and moved to Detroit.

2 TINKERING

Henry studied new inventions in
Detroit. He read articles in
magazines such as *Scientific American* and
World of Science. One article left a big
impression on him. It described a new kind
of engine. A German man named Nikolaus
A. Otto had built the engine. It ran on gas
instead of coal. It produced power by
burning a mixture of gas and air.

After three years in Detroit, Henry heard some exciting news. His father's neighbor had bought a Westinghouse steam engine. The man wanted Henry to run it for him. The nineteen-year-old happily agreed. He returned to the farm. Henry soon mastered the engine. He became so skilled with it that Westinghouse hired him to repair their machines.

Henry kept tinkering in his free time. He built his own steam-powered tractor. He got the machine to move about forty feet before it broke down.

But machines weren't the only thing on Henry's mind. On New Year's Eve 1885, Henry went to a dance. There he met a girl named Clara Jane Bryant. Henry fell in love with the chestnut-haired beauty. Clara saw that there was something special about the serious young man with the pale gray eyes. Three years later, in April 1888, they married.

Clara Jane Bryant was the daughter of a wealthy farmer.

Henry's father gave the couple a farm to live on. Henry kept tinkering. He'd given up steam engines. He thought gas-powered engines were the way of the future. But he realized he didn't have the knowledge to build a gas engine on his own. He needed to learn more about electricity. Electricity helps gas engines run.

Henry took a job with the Edison Illuminating Company in Detroit. He knew he could learn about electricity there. Thomas Edison, the famous inventor, owned the company. It supplied electricity for many homes and businesses in Detroit.

Henry Ford (BACK ROW, THIRD FROM RIGHT) and other employees of the Edison Illuminating Company in 1892.

A LITTLE TOO SMART

Henry's first job in Detroit was with a company that made streetcars. These cars ran through cities on rails. Henry was fired after just six days. He never explained what happened. But he hinted that he may have been too smart for his own good. A group of mechanics had spent hours trying to solve a problem. They had no luck. Then sixteen-year-old Henry stepped in. He fixed the problem in just a few minutes. He made the older mechanics look foolish. They showed him the door.

Henry stayed with the Edison company for nearly ten years. Yet he didn't spend a lot of time actually working for the business. He fixed problems and repaired machines when needed. But he spent most of his days working on his own inventions. He was determined to build a gas-powered engine.

One night, Henry's work paid off. It was Christmas Eve 1893. Clara was making a holiday meal for the family. Henry brought his engine into the kitchen. He clamped it to the sink. Clara dripped gasoline into the machine. Henry turned a wheel, and the engine roared to life.

Henry was thrilled. Clara was excited too. But she was afraid the noise would wake up their newborn son, Edsel, who was sleeping in the next room.

3 EARLY MORNING DRIVE

Henry didn't celebrate for long. He knew his engine was too small to be useful. He spent the next two years trying to build a bigger engine. "Every night . . . I worked on the new motor," said Henry. "I cannot say that it was hard work. No work [that you enjoy] is ever hard."

Henry had help building his engine. In fact, he often didn't work much at all. He surrounded himself with a group of friends. Henry gave instructions. His friends followed them.

Most of the time, the team worked in a brick shed behind the Ford home. Sometimes they worked in the basement of the Edison Illuminating Company. As the engine came together, the men also built a four-wheeled carriage. The engine would power this vehicle.

This replica, or copy, of Henry's backyard shed shows where Henry and his friends worked on their engine.

The carriage was called the Quadricycle. It had four bicycle wheels. Its engine rested under a small seat. On June 4, 1896, the machine was ready for a test drive. Clara was there to watch and help. So was James Bishop. He was a friend of the Fords.

But as Henry was about to roll the machine out of the shed, he realized he had made a terrible mistake. The Quadricycle was too wide to fit through the door! So Henry grabbed an ax. Clara and James looked on while Henry knocked out some bricks to widen the door.

Henry sits in his Quadricycle in 1896.

HENRY'S QUADRICYCLE

Henry's first vehicle was very simple. Its engine produced just four horsepower. (Horsepower is a unit used to measure an engine's power.) A modern lawn mower engine produces about six horsepower. The Quadricycle had no steering wheel. Instead, the driver steered by moving a long bar called a tiller. The Quadricycle had two speed settings—ten miles per hour and twenty miles per hour—and no brakes.

At last, the Quadricycle was ready for its first run. It was four in the morning. Henry started the machine without trouble. Then he hopped on and headed into Detroit. James rode ahead on a bike to clear the streets. The Quadricycle broke down just once. Henry and James had to push the machine to the Edison plant to replace a part. But soon, the machine was running again, and Henry rode home.

Henry parked the machine in the damaged shed. "We both went to bed for a few winks of sleep," James recalled. "We soon woke up, had a bite of breakfast . . . and then [went] to the Edison plant to report to work just as if nothing unusual happened." Henry was thrilled with his success. But he was already thinking about building a bigger car.

4 CRAZY HENRY

Henry and his Quadricycle became a common sight on the streets of Detroit. "Everyone thought Henry was crazier than heck with that darned car of his," said a family acquaintance. "They used to say, 'Here comes that crazy Henry Ford.'"

But "Crazy Henry" had a plan. He kept working and learning. He built more powerful cars.

Meanwhile, a car craze was gripping the nation. More and more cars were appearing on city streets. People called them horseless carriages. Some folks thought cars were just a fad. Others, like Henry, knew that they were the future.

Henry (RIGHT) knew cars would replace horses. He worked hard to improve his Quadricycle.

Car races were a big part of the horseless carriage craze. Americans loved the new sport of auto racing. Henry decided to build his own race car. He hoped to earn fame by beating other cars on the track.

His car was ready to go by the summer of 1901. On October 10, Henry entered the car in a race at the Grosse Pointe racetrack, near Detroit. He was up against Alexander Winton, of Cleveland, Ohio. Alexander was the most famous racer of the day. Thousands gathered to watch the race.

Henry (LEFT) and a friend sit in his 1901 race car called SWEEPSTAKES.

Alexander took an early lead. Henry had never raced a car before. But he still kept up with his rival. Henry's friend Spider Huff rode along. Spider leaned out of the car when they turned corners. This helped to keep the car from tipping over.

The cars traveled at about forty-five miles per hour—very fast for the time. As the end of the race neared, Alexander's engine began to have problems. The crowd went wild as Henry sped past to victory!

THE *ARROW* AND THE *999*

In 1902, Henry built a pair of race cars. They were called the *Arrow* and the *999*.
Henry hired a bicycle racer, Barney Oldfield, to drive the *999*. In October 1902, Barney won a big race in Ohio. In January 1904, Henry himself tried to break the world speed record in the *Arrow*. Driving on frozen Lake Saint Clair near Detroit, Henry broke the record with a speed of more than ninety miles per hour.

News of the race spread. Henry became famous. He liked the fame. But he didn't like racing. "I was scared to death, and I'll never do that again," he told a friend. He decided to stick to building cars. He hired others to do the racing for him.

Henry's fame led to a new business. On June 16, 1903, Henry founded the Ford Motor Company. Ford's first car was the Model A. It sold well. Soon Ford was working on a better car. It was called the Model B. By 1908, Ford was one of the top automakers in the country. Ford cars were known for their quality.

Henry's company built many different car models. He took his son, Edsel, for a ride in the 1905 Model F.

By 1908, cars were becoming even more common. But they were too expensive for most people. Henry didn't think this was fair. He thought everyone should have a chance to enjoy cars. He decided to build an affordable car. "No man making a good salary will be unable to own one," he promised.

Henry's promise became real in 1908. That year, Henry made a car called the Model T. The car was a wonder. It was fun to drive. It rarely broke down. Best of all, it cost just $850. Most cars cost at least twice as much.

The 1908 Model T (ABOVE) was a very popular car. It was the first car that most Americans could afford.

The Model T was a huge hit. Ford built more than ten thousand in the car's first year of production. But people wanted even more. So Henry built a larger Ford factory. Michigan's Highland Park plant opened in 1910. By 1913, the plant was building half of the new cars in the United States.

But Highland Park still couldn't build enough Model Ts. The cars took a long time to make. Teams of workers built them by hand, one at a time. It took a team twelve and a half hours to build just one car. Henry was always trying to come up with a way to speed up the process.

Thousands of employees of the Ford Motor Company stand in front of the Highland Park plant in 1913.

In April 1913, a Ford engineer tried using an assembly line in the plant. Each worker had one job to do. One worker would install one car part. Then he passed the part down the line. The next worker would install a different piece.

The assembly line was a great time-saver. By October, the Highland Park plant was using assembly lines to build every part of the Model T. Separate assembly lines built separate parts of the car. Then these parts were added to the new cars as they rolled down the main assembly lines. It took workers just under six hours to build a car.

A Model T comes down the assembly line at the Ford Motor Company factory in 1914.

Ford assembly lines built all of these car frames in just one day.

The assembly lines began to work even better over time. By 1914, Ford workers could build a Model T in just over an hour and a half. The company built more than 300,000 cars that year. By 1916, the number had jumped to more than 585,000.

Soon other car companies were copying Ford's assembly line. Makers of other kinds of goods followed. Assembly lines sped up the process of making boats, tin cans, toys, and just about everything else.

Assembly lines not only sped up production. They also made it cheaper to put products together. It cost Ford a lot less money to build its cars on assembly lines. As a result, Henry was able to lower the price of his cars. By 1916, the Model T cost just $360. A few years later, the price would drop to $250. Henry had built a car that almost everyone could afford. But he wasn't done yet.

The Model T's price decreased over the years. Owning a car became more and more common.

5 FOLK HERO

By the late 1910s, even Highland Park's assembly lines couldn't make Model Ts fast enough. Henry was already working on plans for an even larger Ford plant. The new factory would be along the Rouge River near Dearborn.

Henry's factory took the assembly line to a new level. The River Rouge plant soon became the largest factory in the world. It was two miles long and three-quarters of a mile wide. More than one hundred thousand people worked there.

Through it all, Henry became one of the most famous—and richest—men in the world. His Model T made him a hero to millions of people. Henry's car had changed their lives. It helped farmers do their work. It allowed them to pick up supplies or to visit the city for a night on the town.

The River Rouge plant is one of the world's most famous auto factories.

FORDISM

Before the River Rouge plant opened, the Ford company bought most of its materials from other businesses. But the River Rouge plant had many of its own supplies. This kept the price of the Model T down.

The River Rouge plant's affordable methods for making cars became known as Fordism. Other businesses copied these methods. They allowed businesses to produce their products more cheaply than ever before.

The Model T gave city folks a chance to explore the country's open spaces. It also gave them the chance to spread out. Millions of Americans began moving to the suburbs. They didn't need to rely on the city's streetcars or their own two feet to get to work. They could move out of crowded cities and enjoy their very own backyards.

Henry enjoyed his fame. He worked hard to stay in the public eye. He was happy to share his ideas about life, business, and health.

Some of Henry's ideas were strange. For example, he thought salt was a key to health. He said people would be healthier if they brushed their teeth with salt and rubbed salt in their hair. He thought colds came from eating too much. He told people with colds not to eat anything for forty-eight hours.

Henry liked the fame his Model T brought him.

Americans loved hearing Henry's ideas. They loved that he was rich but lived simply. Henry didn't like rich people. He didn't spend much time with them. He didn't care for fancy hotels or restaurants. He preferred spending time with Clara and a small group of friends. His favorite pastimes were camping and bird-watching.

Henry enjoyed spending time with his wife, Clara (LEFT).

Henry at the wheel with his friends John Burroughs, a nature writer, and Thomas Edison (IN THE BACK SEAT)

Henry was so popular that many people said he should become a politician. In 1918, he ran for the U.S. Senate. Henry refused to make any speeches. Instead, he let other people sing his praises. Henry lost the election by just a few thousand votes.

In the early 1920s, Henry thought about running for president. Thousands of people sent him letters asking him to run. But Henry decided against it.

Henry had many interests outside of the car business. He spent millions of dollars collecting pieces of history from the United States' past. He opened a museum to put these things on display. It is called the Henry Ford Museum and Greenfield Village. He also spent millions of dollars to build new schools around the country.

Visitors to Greenfield Village can see this model of Henry's father's barn.

In the 1930s, Henry and Clara built a large home in the Georgia countryside. The couple spent a few weeks there every year. Henry was happiest when he was outdoors. He was interested in nature. One of his favorite activities was chopping up logs for firewood.

When the United States entered World War II (1939–1945), Henry took on a new interest. He began supporting the war effort. Henry's company started making weapons to use in the war. Henry didn't like war. But he wanted to help his country so the fighting would end quickly.

Henry (RIGHT) looks at a B-24 bomber plane. His company made these planes during World War II.

Thousands of people came to the Henry Ford Museum after Henry's death to pay their respects.

Henry Ford died on April 7, 1947. About thirty thousand people came to his funeral. Newspaper articles around the world praised Henry. They tried to sum up his incredible life. It wasn't easy. When Henry was born in 1863, the automobile didn't exist. By the time he died, tens of millions of people owned automobiles.

Henry Ford changed the way people traveled. He changed the way they did business. His Model T transformed the car from a luxury into an important tool. Henry Ford put the world on wheels.

TIMELINE

In the year . . .

1879 Henry moved from his father's farm to Detroit.
he was fired from his first job after just six days.   Age 16

1888 he married Clara Jane Bryant.

1891 he took a job at the Edison Illuminating Company in Detroit.

1893 his son, Edsel, was born.
Henry completed his first working gas-powered engine.

1896 he drove his first car, the Quadricycle, for the first time.   Age 32

1901 he defeated Alexander Winton in an exciting race at Grosse Pointe racetrack.

1903 Henry founded the Ford Motor Company.

1904 he broke the world speed record driving the *Arrow* on frozen Lake Saint Clair.

1908 he introduced the Ford Model T.   Age 45

1910 he opened the Highland Park plant on New Year's Day.

1913 his company began using assembly lines to build cars.

1917 his company began building the giant River Rouge plant.

1918 he lost a close race for U.S. senator.   Age 55

1925 his River Rouge plant was completed

1929 he opened the Henry Ford Museum.

1947 he died on April 7.   Age 83

THE HENRY FORD MUSEUM AND GREENFIELD VILLAGE

Henry Ford didn't like how history classes were all about names of important leaders and dates of important events. Henry believed that the best way to teach history was to show what life was like in the past. So in the 1920s, he founded the Henry Ford Museum and Greenfield Village.

The museum's many exhibits include farming tools from different periods of U.S. history. The museum also has a large collection of historic cars. A visit to Greenfield Village is meant to be like traveling into the past. Dozens of famous homes and buildings have been moved from their original locations and rebuilt on the village grounds. They include the house where Henry was born and the laboratory where Henry's friend Thomas Edison invented the lightbulb.

The Henry Ford Museum features a collection of historic cars. Visitors can read about how the cars affected U.S. culture.

45

FURTHER READING

Mara, Wil. *Henry Ford*. New York: Children's Press, 2003.
Read more about Henry Ford in this book about his life.

McCarthy, Pat. *Henry Ford: Building Cars for Everyone*. Berkeley Heights, NJ: Enslow Publishers, 2002. A biography of Henry Ford for young readers.

Mitchell, Barbara. *We'll Race You, Henry: A Story about Henry Ford*. Minneapolis: Carolrhoda Books, Inc., 1986. An illustrated book about the adventures of young Henry Ford.

Zemlicka, Shannon. *Thomas Edison*. Minneapolis: Lerner Publications Company, 2004. Learn more about the life of one of Henry Ford's best friends, the great inventor Thomas Edison.

WEBSITES

Ford Motor Company
http://www.ford.com The website of the Ford Motor Company has information on the company's newest cars as well as information about the company's history.

The Henry Ford Museum and Greenfield Village
http://www.hfmgv.org Visit the official website of Henry's museum, and view online exhibits and much more.

SELECT BIBLIOGRAPHY

Banham, Russ. *The Ford Century: Ford Motor Company and the Innovations That Shaped the World*. New York: Artisan, 2002.

Brinkley, Douglas. *Wheels for the World: Henry Ford, His Company, and a Century of Progress*. New York: Viking, 2003.

Cabadas, Joseph P. *River Rouge: Ford's Industrial Colossus*. Saint Paul: Motorbooks International, 2004.

Collier, Peter, and David Horowitz. *The Fords: An American Epic*. San Francisco: Encounter Books, 2002.

Ford, Henry, and Samuel Crowther. *My Life and Work*. Whitefish, MT: Kessinger Publishing, 2003.

Watts, Steven. *The People's Tycoon: Henry Ford and the American Century*. New York: Alfred A. Knopf, 2005.

INDEX

Acknowledgments

The images in this book are used with permission of: © Getty Images, pp. 4, 37; From the Collections of The Henry Ford, pp. 7 (both), 8, 14, 15, 20, 26, 30, 32, 35, 42; The Art Archive/London Studio Paris/Dagli Orti, p. 10; The Art Archive/Musée National de la voiture et du tourisme Compiégne/Dagli Orti, p. 11; © Hulton Archive/Getty Images, pp. 16, 21, 31; © Spencer Arnold/Getty Images, p. 25; © AFP/AFP/Getty Images, p. 28; © Three Lions/Getty Images, pp. 29, 33; Library of Congress (LC-DIG-ggbain-20410), p. 38; © Bettmann/CORBIS, pp. 39, 41; © Keystone/Getty Images, p. 40; © Layne Kennedy/CORBIS, p. 45.

Front Cover: Library of Congress (LC-USZ62-111278)
Back Cover: Courtesy of the National Automobile Museum (The Harrah Collection)

For quoted material: pp. 7, 19, 29, Steven Watts, *The People's Tycoon: Henry Ford and the American Century* (New York: Alfred A. Knopf, 2005); pp. 8 (both), 9 (top), 23, 28, Douglas Brinkley, *Wheels for the World: Henry Ford, His Company, and a Century of Progress* (New York: Penguin Books, 2003); pp. 9 (bottom), 10, 11, 12, Henry Ford and Samuel Crowther, *My Life and Work* (Whitefish, MT: Kessinger Publishing, 2003); p. 24, Peter Collier and David Horowitz, *The Fords: An American Epic* (San Francisco: Encounter Books, 2002).